Built to SucSEED

TREE LIFE

Copyright © 2023 by Dr. Darius Jerome Williams

Published by Arrows and Stones

All rights reserved. No portion of this book may be reproduced, stored in a retrieval system, or transmitted in any form or by any means—electronic, mechanical, photocopy, recording, scanning, or other—except for brief quotations in critical reviews or articles, without prior written permission of the author.

Scripture quotations marked ESV are from The ESV® Bible (The Holy Bible, English Standard Version®), copyright © 2001 by Crossway, a publishing ministry of Good News Publishers. Used by permission. All rights reserved. | Scripture quotations marked KJV are taken from the King James Version of the Bible. Public domain. | Scripture quotations marked NIV are taken from the Holy Bible, New International Version®, NIV®. Copyright © 1973, 1978, 1984, 2011 by Biblica, Inc.™ Used by permission of Zondervan. All rights reserved worldwide. www.zondervan.com. The "NIV" and "New International Version" are trademarks registered in the United States Patent and Trademark Office by Biblica, Inc.™ | Scripture quotations marked NKJV are taken from the New King James Version®. Copyright © 1982 by Thomas Nelson. Used by permission. All rights reserved.

For foreign and subsidiary rights, contact the author.

Cover design by: Greg Mckinney

ISBN: 978-1-962401-34-0   1 2 3 4 5 6 7 8 9 10

Printed in the United States of America

Built to SucSEED
TREE LIFE

DR. DARIUS WILLIAMS

ARROWS & STONES

"He is like a tree planted by streams of water that yields its fruit in its season, and its leaf does not wither. In all that he does, he prospers."
—Psalm 1:3 (ESV)

CONTENTS

Foreword .... *ix*

Preface .... *xi*

Acknowledgments .... *xiii*

Introduction 15

CHAPTER 1. **Growing in a Dark Place** 17

CHAPTER 2. **What's in a Seed** 23

CHAPTER 3. **Check Your Roots** 31

CHAPTER 4. **Watch Your Fruit** 41

CHAPTER 5. **Don't Be Caught Without Fruit** 49

CHAPTER 6. **Pain to Growth** 55

CHAPTER 7. **What's Growing in Your Garden?** 63

CHAPTER 8. **Suckers** 69

CHAPTER 9. **Built to SucSeed** 79

About the Author 87

FOREWORD

Dr. Darius Williams is one of the most prolific communicators of the revelatory word of God I have ever met, and can pray the house down like few others as a mighty warrior intercessor. But even more than all of the amazing gifts of God within his design that I am proud to mention, he is my friend and a spiritual son, and I am honored to have walked with him for many years now. He always manages to bring the awe of God into every room and this book is no different. *Built to SucSeed* is not only packed full of the wisdom of the Spirit of God, but it carries within its pages some very crucial truths that are in perfect timing with what God is doing in the Earth in this very hour. The Father is raising up His sons and daughters and imparting to them His principles for transformation and reformation. We know this anointed life of Christ comes as a result of understanding the Father and His design for our lives, for others, and for creation. This concept is still fairly new territory for believers and this book will help you to grab hold of this new paradigm and will cause you to better understand where you are in your own journey, as well as where the church is and why. We are called to unearth God's glorious treasures within our own lives and everything around us, even creation. So, let the Spirit of God create a masterpiece in you and everything you touch as you yield to His process in this hour and dive into the deep and practical revelation Darius expresses so well in *Built to SucSeed*.

—Kent Mattox
Founder of Word Alive International Outreach

PREFACE

I consider this book as my second published work, although my initial foray into writing was my dissertation. Yet, this work holds a distinct place in my heart because it marks the beginning of a journey into a realm of literary creations that I hope will continue to grow.

It all began right before I embarked on the incredible journey of marriage, in the quiet town of Pell City, Alabama. It was a simple vision, yet its significance took years to fully reveal itself. I stood outside my home one day and saw something quite extraordinary. In the vast expanse of the sky, there it was—a wall plug, suspended seemingly in midair. Across the top and bottom of this ethereal plug, titles and scriptures flashed in a mesmerizing rhythm. I watched, transfixed by the message it conveyed.

That vision stayed with me, etched in my memory as a tantalizing mystery waiting to unfold. It wasn't until a half-decade later that God began to unveil His plan. He promised to grant me revelations—profound understandings of scripture that would be both impactful and transformative. With His guidance, I embarked on a journey of writing, putting pen to paper to share the insights I'd received.

My focus? The intricate relationship between the elements of creation and the spirit that binds them all. God's creation, I discovered, was no random act but a deliberate and purposeful masterpiece. There existed a profound connection, an unspoken law, a principle, a rule that underpinned every relationship between the elements of His creation.

The pages of this book are dedicated to unveiling the revelations bestowed upon me by the Holy Spirit. I will delve into the intricate tapestry of the relationship between the majestic trees and the enigmatic entity that is mankind. Through this exploration, we will uncover profound similarities and lessons, peeling back the layers of creation's intricate design.

ACKNOWLEDGMENTS

As I reflect upon my journey and the blessings that have graced my life, I feel compelled to express my gratitude to those who have played significant roles in my existence. There is a gallery of individuals who have contributed to the person I am today, and I wish to acknowledge them.

First and foremost, my wife, Rebecca Williams, who has been my unwavering support and my partner in all of life's adventures. Your love and companionship have been my greatest treasures. Next in line are my precious children: Kailynn, Karis, and Kaslee. The three of you have filled my life with immeasurable joy, teaching me valuable lessons about love, patience, and the wonders of parenthood.

My heartfelt gratitude extends to my mother, Sonya Williams, whose anointing to overcome obstacles has shaped my character and nurtured my spirit. You have been a perfect example that our past never predicts our future, but instead helps us succeed in it. In remembrance, I honor the memory of my grandmothers, Mary Lee Scott and Betty Sue "Mae Joe" Williams Coggins. Their wisdom and love have left an indelible mark on my heart, reminding me of the importance of family and heritage.

I cannot overlook the influence of my pastor, Timothy E. Caldwell, whose spiritual leadership has guided me on my faith journey. Your teachings have been a source of inspiration and growth in my life. Lastly, I owe a debt of gratitude to my spiritual father, Kent, who has provided me with wisdom, mentorship, and a spiritual compass. Your influence has been transformative, leading me on a path of deeper understanding and purpose. The constant impartation, spaces, opportunities, and push have helped form me into a kingdom leader unlike any before.

I have to shout out to my graphic designer Greg Mckinney. If you have not worked with Greg, I would recommend him over anyone. You are a creative genius. To my Word Center church family, I love you beyond measure, and wouldn't choose to fulfill purpose with any other body of believers.

These individuals are the cornerstones of my life, and I am forever grateful for their presence and influence. Their love, support, and guidance have enriched my existence and made me the person I am today.

INTRODUCTION

In the Bible, trees hold significant symbolism and play a crucial role in the relationship between God, humanity, and the natural world. From the very beginning, trees are depicted as essential elements of creation, intricately woven into the narrative of human existence. In the book of Genesis, the tree of life and the tree of the knowledge of good and evil are prominently featured in the Garden of Eden. God placed Adam and Eve in this paradise, providing them with an abundance of trees and fruits to sustain and delight them. However, He forbade them from eating the fruit of the tree of the knowledge of good and evil, emphasizing the importance of obedience and trust in their relationship with Him.

Sadly, Adam and Eve succumbed to temptation and ate from the forbidden tree, elevating man's belief in the voice of the serpent above that of Elohim. One of the main things that separate man from God is not sin; it is his lack of belief in God. I know one may struggle with this concept, but Salvation happens as a result of man choosing to verbally confess his belief in God. This signifies that reconciliation happens not just when we ask for forgiveness and turn from our wicked ways, but when we choose to elevate our belief in what God said above any other voice. The event in the garden demonstrates the profound impact of human choices and highlights the significance of trees as markers of moral and spiritual decision-making.

Throughout the Bible, trees continue to hold symbolic meaning. The Psalms compare the righteous person to a tree planted by streams of water, whose leaf does not wither. This imagery emphasizes the importance of seeking nourishment from God's Word and cultivating a life rooted in righteousness and trust. In the New Testament, Jesus refers to Himself as the true vine, and His followers as branches. This analogy highlights the interconnectedness between believers and Christ, emphasizing the need for spiritual sustenance and dependence on Him. Trees are also used metaphorically to describe the fruits of the Spirit, such as love, joy, peace, and kindness.

Furthermore, Jesus's crucifixion on a wooden cross underscores the relationship between trees and humanity's redemption. The cross represents the ultimate sacrifice made for the salvation of humanity, demonstrating God's immense love and grace. In various passages, trees are associated with healing, provision, and restoration. In the book of Ezekiel, the vision of the river flowing from the temple describes trees whose leaves bring healing to the nations. The imagery of a fruitful tree also appears in the book of Revelation, symbolizing the ultimate restoration of creation and the eternal presence of God.

Chapter 1

GROWING IN A DARK PLACE

> *"And God said, Let the earth bring forth grass, the herb yielding seed, and the fruit tree yielding fruit after his kind, whose seed is in itself, upon the earth: and it was so."*
> —Genesis 1:11 (KJV)

I grew up in a low socio-economic status home, with a single parent (Mom), in a low-income housing complex. All I knew growing up was school, playing with neighborhood kids, and church. My grandmother, who is really my great-aunt, made sure that all of her grandchildren attended church. We also participated in all youth-related ministries, activities, and programs. I was in the youth choir, a part of youth Sunday school, leader of the youth step team, dance team, and the list goes on. I eventually became the leader of most youth activities within my childhood church. Little did I know that my grandmother was making sure that I had seeds planted in me while I was young. Eventually, what she knew that I didn't know was that those seeds would eventually grow into fruit trees.

All trees originate from a seed. All seeds have to be sown in order to grow. There is a law that God created between the soil and seed that you must understand. Oftentimes, we judge a seed by its ending place and never consider the process it took to get where it is. We enjoy apples, oranges, and bananas; however, we don't consider their process to become fruit. All seeds go into the ground. This means their first stop is down, dark, and hard. You see, for many of us, life doesn't start off in the best possible circumstance or situation, nor do we have everything we could ever ask for. Most of us would not say that life has been easy. Most of us start off in a dark place that is hard... and lonely.

We are not aware or have a clear idea of what our life's purpose is. Just like the seed, we all can admit to feeling like we were underground and couldn't see what was next. You cannot tell the seed's next place by looking at where it started. If you judge your next place by your current place or by where you started, you may end up discouraged.

A seed is buried first. Being buried and trees may seem like an odd pair, but they share an intricate connection that speaks to the cycle of life and nature's enduring wisdom. When we talk about being buried, it's often in the context of death, where our physical bodies return to the earth. In this act, we're not only relinquishing our mortal coil but also offering ourselves back to the very ground that nurtured us, in a sense. It's a profound act of giving, an acknowledgment of our brief existence in the grand scheme of things.

A seed has to go underground because it must hit rock bottom before it even starts to grow. We complain about landing on the bottom, but the bottom is the best place to be in. When you are walking in God, you can never use where you are as a determinant for where you will be next. Some of you may feel like you are at rock bottom now; others can recall when they were there. When you are at your lowest, I have a word for you: **There's nowhere to go from there but UP!**

> **YOU CAN'T HAVE A NEW LIFE WITHOUT GIVING UP YOUR OLD LIFE.**

According to the Word, in Romans 12:1, we must die daily. You have to present your bodies as a living sacrifice. We must be crucified with Christ, which means that your first order of business—if you are going to walk with God—is that you must be willing to bury yourself. You have to give yourself a decent burial in order to walk in the newness of God. We know the Word says old things are passed away, and behold all things become new. We too, like a seed, must go down, be buried in a dark place, and give up our life in order to grow into the man/woman God created us to be. You can't have a new life without giving up your old life.

When the moment of my salvation arrived, a profound transformation took place. It ceased to be merely my life; instead, it became HIS life. My declaration of love for God wasn't a mere string of words; it was my heart earnestly expressing its deep affection for the One who loved me first. Now, a pivotal choice looms before the body of Christ, a decision to be made today: Whom shall we serve?

This is why the church must undergo a spiritual rebirth, for only through a true death can something be resurrected. In the context of resurrection, it means being raised and given a new body. God is striving to construct a new body, known as the remnant. The sole path to becoming a remnant is to be raised, and the only way to be raised is through a proper death and a proper burial.

What's proper, you might ask? Proper burial signifies that the deceased person is permanently removed from this world. When they are placed in the ground and covered with earth, they are forever separated from the realm of this earthly life. That's why, as Paul puts it, "You have not only died to it; you have been buried to it" (Romans 6:4, author paraphrase). **Returning to a life of sin after joining with Christ is akin to unearthing a long-buried corpse.** Most times, the most difficult thing for a person is to sacrifice their will, let alone their life. GOD WANTS ALL OF YOU! It is hard for to be DISCIPLED by Christ when you haven't even agreed to the first terms yet: DENY YOURSELF and follow Him. We claim to follow Him for real, but we never left anything to do it. If your journey of following God hasn't required you to surrender anything, I regret to inform you that you might not be following Christ at all. In reality, you might still be steadfastly treading your own path, just as you always have, and merely visiting the presence of Christ.

So, a seed is buried, but what the seed comes to know is, once it hits rock bottom, the only way out is to open up. A seed must break open and give up its contents on the inside before it will start growing. "***Ephphatha!***" Translated open up or to be opened (see Mark 7:34). Once the seed is broken, and it opens up, then the law of the soil and seed begins to take place. We must understand that like the seed, God has to break us so that we will open and yield the contents that were placed in us from our genesis. Stop and take a moment and tell yourself "*Ephphatha*". It means to be open. ***You have to open up!*** There are valuable contents, skills, gifts, talents, information, and knowledge—among many other things—that you have from God that the Earth needs.

We have many days on Earth, but the Bible says they are filled with trouble. There are seasons that are very difficult for us. The moments in your life when you thought God wasn't with you, around you, or listening to your prayers may have been moments where He was causing the seed in you to open up. You have substance on the inside of you that is waiting to grow, mature, and reveal itself to the world. Sometimes the only person that keeps us from growing is ourselves. We fail to open up to GOD. It is sad that oftentimes it takes terrible situations for us to get close to HIM. God gave me a word one day that has been encouraging me ever since. If and when you feel like you are in a dark place, God said,

"Seeds grow first in the dark."

There's a simple prophetic word for you. When you are living the tree life, you can't trust your own eyes to know what it is you are supposed to do. This is because it is dark in your first place of growth. However, you must trust that in this place, God is fine-tuning your spirit to discern what is right.

You can discern more with your spirit than you can see with your eyes.

You can't trust your natural eyes in any season. There are times, as a seed, you will not even see yourself growing, but you must discern your growth. You have to let your discernment become your eyes.

I hope that you are being filled with revelation and encouraged at the same time. I want you to realize that the place you are in, even if it is dark, is not necessarily a bad place. God has more for you. Many times, we fight against going through difficult times in our lives. We complain, bicker, stop going to church, stop praying, stop reading, stop functioning in the kingdom because we feel like we are in a dry place. I call this a dry place; some say a "low place", and others just simply say bad place. Many times, we suffer an identity crisis. However, we must realize that we find our identity in the crisis. The place you are in is the place where the seed finds out what is really on the inside of it. We figure out what we are made of and what God put in us, thereby I'm suggesting that **we do some of our most powerful growing in a dark place.** Yes, I said it, in the place where you don't think you are growing, you are probably growing the most.

Chapter 2

WHAT'S IN A SEED

"Except a corn of wheat fall into the ground ... it abideth alone."
—John 12:24, KJV

Just as all trees originate from seed, so too does the correlation between fruit seeds and mankind hold great significance in the biblical narrative. Seeds possess a profound wisdom, reflecting the intricate design of creation itself. In the same way, humanity, formed in the image of God, carries within them the potential for growth, purpose, and bearing fruit. In the book of Genesis, God commanded the earth to bring forth vegetation, each with the ability to reproduce after its own kind. This divine order speaks to the remarkable nature of seeds, which contain the blueprint for future life. Similarly, God breathed life into Adam, infusing him with His own image and likeness. Thus, every human being possesses a seed of divinity within him, a potential waiting to be realized.

Just as seeds require specific conditions for growth, humanity also thrives when nurtured in the right environment. In the Psalms, the righteous are compared to trees planted by streams of water, drawing nourishment and strength. Likewise, believers find sustenance and spiritual growth when they abide in God's presence, immersing themselves in His Word and communing with Him through prayer. Moreover, the New Testament speaks of the fruits of the Spirit, which manifest in the lives of those who are connected to Christ, the true vine. Galatians 5:22-23 (NIV) states, "But the fruit of the Spirit is love, joy, peace, forbearance, kindness, goodness, faithfulness, gentleness, and self-control." These fruits exemplify the transformative power of God's presence within us, shaping our character and influencing our interactions with others.

God placed the seed of the tree in the fruit. A fruit tree that does not produce fruit will never produce more trees. A fruitless fruit tree can look strong, tall, and full of leaves, but it has no legacy because it failed to reproduce the seed that it received to create itself. A fruitless tree is selfish and a poor testimony. The true prosperity of the tree comes when the tree produces fruit for others to enjoy and for the reproduction of more trees. **The tree never complains about being used, neither does it withhold the fruit because of the receiver of the tree.** Trees don't get to determine who benefits from what it has to offer. However, all who are willing to partake, and receive its fruit are the ones who will benefit from it.

"Except a corn of wheat fall into the ground . . . it abideth alone."
—John 12:24, KJV

Just as a seed must be sown in order to grow, humanity is called to sow seeds of kindness, compassion, and love in the world. As Jesus proclaimed, "Very truly I tell you, unless a kernel of wheat falls to the ground and dies, it remains only a single seed. But if it dies, it produces many seeds" (John 12:24, NIV). This principle of self-sacrifice echoes the concept of dying to oneself, surrendering personal desires and ambitions in service to others. By doing so, we become instruments of God's love, sowing seeds of transformation that bear fruit in the lives of those we encounter.

Listen! God wants us to bear fruit; as a matter of fact, I believe the word says *much* fruit. However, you will never find within yourself what it takes to remain fruitful. It is God who provides the necessary things for fruit to continue to be reproduced in our lives. The Word says it is our job to plant the seed but God's job to water it. I know you want to cause it to grow, but you can't. Some of us are not as fruitful as we desire because we are too busy trying to make it happen ourselves. You can't build a name for yourself, nor can you make yourself famous, but it is God that says I will make your name great.

Quick testimony. I have been in education for seventeen years. When I was ready to make the transition from the classroom into a leadership position as a principal, I was going on interviews left and right. I worked hard on my resume, building relationships, networking, and attempting to get my name before the right people. I interviewed in 2011 and I was offered the job but wasn't released from my current contract. Therefore, I couldn't take the promotion. In 2012, I did it again, interviewed, and was offered a job in another city. This time, my wife and I went and looked for potential places to live in this new city, but before it was finalized, I received a call saying that, all of a sudden, they had to go in another direction.

> **YOUR RELATIONSHIP WITH HIM WILL DETERMINE THE QUALITY OF WHAT IS PRODUCED OUT OF YOU.**

I began to get upset with God, upset with friends, and frustrated that it wasn't working in my favor. Then God spoke to me and said, *"Let me promote you!"* You have to be careful with self-promotion because it can't be trusted. I kept telling God that it was going to delay the timeline of the goals I had set for my life. God said, "I am God, and I am not in time, time is in Me." I didn't understand that statement until a couple of years later. In 2013, the following year, I was offered a promotion to Assistant Principal and was able to accept the position. Typically, you have to be an assistant for three years before you get the chance to become a principal. However, the following year in 2014, a superintendent called me and asked me to come and be the principal of my old high school. I was in awe! God said I can do in a year what would have taken you three years. God doesn't need your timeline; He has one of his own. "For I know the thoughts and plans I have for you . . . to bring you to an expected end (Jeremiah 29:11, author paraphrase).

Long story short, we need to work less on building our brand, and more on building our relationship with God. Your relationship with Him will determine the quality of what is produced out of you. If you are a singer, I don't want your gift to be perfect—and not anointed. It is the anointing that destroys the yoke. Sometimes we work to get to perfection when we should put more effort into perfecting our alignment with the Spirit of God. When we submit to the Spirit of God, the anointing flows, and lives are changed. If we are going to impact the Earth with our gifts, we can't do it without God having an impact on us first. What am I saying? ***You can't be impactful until you have been first impacted.***

We don't discover what is really in us until we discover the one who placed it there. God says through the prophet Jeremiah that before He formed us in our mothers' wombs, He knew us (see 1:5). Before you were created, your purpose existed. You were created because of purpose. God saw a need in the Earth, then he created us as the solution to the need and placed us on the Earth to fulfill that purpose. Can I tell you something? You are the solution to a problem that you haven't discovered yet! You mean something to somebody, you are important, you are needed, and you are gifted. Stop focusing on what you are not and concentrate on growing what you know yourself to be.

Which means that seed is what grants God access to the Earth. When Mary was impregnated by the HOLY SPIRIT, she received Jesus (the WORD in FLESH), as a seed into her womb. The seed she received was the solution to save mankind. If Mary had aborted Christ because of the way she was impregnated, then she would have prevented God from having access to provide the solution in the Earth. I'm not one for controversial topics, but every time a woman is impregnated with child, a portal is opened in the Earth that gives Heaven access to it. Regardless of how you feel about when a seed becomes a person, it doesn't matter, because what matters is whoever aborts a child has rejected a solution from heaven to Earth. It makes me wonder how many solutions Earth has rejected that could have saved someone's life, made something easier, or maybe even developed the cure to cancer.

I know there are situations that make people want to not bring forth something that could be conceived out of pain, trauma, and without consent. However, there are a lot of children on Earth who were conceived, and the mother wanted to abort. Some of whom ended up changing the world, cities, systems, lives, and circumstances of millions over time. Remember that the seed of the womb brings a solution in the future.

As I live in God, I discover more and more amazing talents and skills that He has given me. I am a seed in the Earth, but I must discover my kind, so that I can find where I belong. I wanted to be a lawyer throughout my entire childhood. I went to college and majored in English pre-law, only to graduate and God tell me that He called me to teach. I asked Him privately, *why did You wait four years, let me graduate, only to tell me that I am destined to be an educator?* In my spirit, I heard God say, "you never asked me."

God is waiting on us to ask Him why we are here; he wants us to discover our purpose. Many of us never ask, or like me, sometimes we take too long to ask. The Word of God says, "Ask and it will be given to you; seek and you will find, knock and the door will be opened to you" (Matthew 7:7, NIV). We need to start teaching our children, friends, colleagues, and people we are connected to that it is more important to seek God early in life so that we can avoid some of the frustrations in life. There is a spiritual development component missing from American homes these days. The Bible speaks about a generation arising that knew not the Lord. We are living in a time when this generation was never introduced to church. Their parents rarely went to church, and as a result, many of the spiritual components that should have been gained throughout their adolescent years of life are not present.

> **THE TREASURE CHEST OF GOD'S GRACE IS NOT AN EXTERNAL QUEST BUT AN INWARD EXPEDITION, WAITING FOR THE MOMENT WE UNLOCK ITS FULL POTENTIAL.**

We are living in a society where perspective is ruled by cultural upbringings instead of the Holy Spirit. *God is after our perspective; He is after the way you see things.* When God can change the way you see, then you will begin to see what is in you. For when the Almighty succeeds in altering the lens through which you view life, an extraordinary revelation awaits you. In this pivotal moment, you'll discover what has been concealed within your very essence. You see, you are not merely a passive entity; you are a seed, a vessel of untapped potential. Your existence is purpose-built for triumph, designed to harbor all that you were destined to become.

Ephesians, the sacred text, affirms this profound truth. In the inspired words of Paul, we are gently reminded of our divine heritage. Every spiritual blessing, every precious gift that we could ever require, resides within us. The treasure chest of God's grace is not an external quest but an inward expedition, waiting for the moment we unlock its full potential.

You are a seed! Built to succeed, housing everything that you were meant to become. As you journey through this book, embrace the profound shift in perspective that God intends for you. It's a transformation that will not only unveil your true identity but also lead you to the boundless blessings hidden within your soul.

Chapter 3

CHECK YOUR ROOTS

"Rooted and built up in him [Christ], and established in the faith."
—Colossians 2:7, NKJV

In the Scriptures, roots are often used metaphorically to illustrate important spiritual concepts. The book of Jeremiah describes the blessed person as being "like a tree planted by water, that sends out its roots by the stream" (Jeremiah 17:8, NIV). This imagery emphasizes the importance of seeking a connection with God, the ultimate source of life and nourishment. Just as the roots of a tree draw from the soil to receive water and nutrients, mankind is invited to tap into the wellspring of God's love, wisdom, and grace.

Furthermore, in his letter to the Ephesians, the apostle Paul encourages believers to be rooted and grounded in love (see Ephesians 3:17). This exhortation highlights the significance of establishing a firm foundation in the love of Christ. By nurturing our relationship with God and anchoring ourselves in His love, we can grow spiritually, being strengthened and established in our faith. Your life will be the result of what or who you are connected to.

The roots of a tree also serve as an anchor, providing stability and support. Similarly, mankind finds stability and security when rooted in God's truth. In the book of Colossians, Paul urges believers to be "rooted and built up in him [Christ] and established in the faith" (Colossians 2:7, NKJV). By grounding ourselves in the teachings of Christ and His Word, we develop a solid foundation that enables us to withstand the storms of life and remain steadfast in our spiritual journey.

Moreover, the image of roots conveys the idea of interconnectedness. In the same way that trees share resources through their root systems, humanity is called to live in unity and community. I view the roots in our lives as the experiences we have had, our teachers, traumas, pain, disappointments, good moments, bad moments, crises, and other things worthy of edging a memory. All these experiences in our lives grow a root connected to an emotion, feeling, thought, belief, and even an action in our hearts. This is because roots are interconnected. The sum total of these memorable experiences, both good and bad, influence one another and dictate the majority of the manifestations in our lives. These manifestations develop into personality, habits, responses, behaviors, actions, attitudes, value systems, character, and even the value of God. It is God's intent for all the things that happen to us to work together for our good, according to Romans 8:28. It doesn't seem like a lot of it is working for our good, and that is because we took away the wrong part of the battle spoil when the war was over.

You must remember there were times in the Bible when God allowed the Israelites to collect the spoils from their victories, and there were times when he told them not to touch a thing or it would defile them. You have to know when it is okay to keep the things that are left over from your warfare. Instead, we are keeping everything, and some of it is causing us grief. In 1 Samuel 15, Saul and his men did not kill the king and take some of the spoils like God had told them to. God got angry because sometimes we fight battles where everything is meant to die and nothing should be kept—and yet, we do. Now think about all the battles you have faced—bad relationships, experiences with people, hurt—and how you walked away from those battles with baggage that God intended for you to kill. Now you have allowed the feelings, emotions, and other roots to take root in your heart. These things affect your ability to walk in divine alignment with the Word of God.

Just as the roots of a tree extend unseen beneath the surface, so too does our spiritual journey often take place in the hidden places of our hearts. The psalmist declares, "Search me, O God, and know my heart! Try me and know my thoughts! And see if there be any grievous way in me and lead me in the way everlasting!" (Psalm 139:23-24, ESV) This prayer reflects the desire to allow God to search the depths of our being, to reveal any areas in need of growth, healing, or transformation. By cultivating a humble and open heart before God, we invite Him to strengthen our roots, nourishing us with His truth and guiding us on the path of righteousness.

All our roots coexist together in places we can't see. They work together whether you want them to or not. The apostle Paul, in his letter to the Corinthians, likens the church to a body, emphasizing the importance of each member functioning together harmoniously (see 1 Corinthians 12:12-27). Just as the roots of trees intertwine and support one another, so too are we called to support, encourage, and uplift one another in our spiritual walk. It is difficult to fulfill this responsibility to one another if we have bad roots in us.

> **JUST AS THE ROOTS OF A TREE EXTEND UNSEEN BENEATH THE SURFACE, SO TOO DOES OUR SPIRITUAL JOURNEY OFTEN TAKE PLACE IN THE HIDDEN PLACES OF OUR HEARTS.**

You have to take care of your roots, water them, and keep them hydrated. It's the water of God that hydrates our souls, not man's generic substitutes. We are enticed out of the will of God when God does not satisfy us. The reason we chase worldly things is because we are thirsty. Jesus told the woman at the well that she was thirsty. You've been drinking, but you are not satisfied because you haven't drunk the right water yet. We may attempt to plant our lives next to a stream of self-sufficiency, only to find ourselves thirsting. It is the water of God's Word that we are to drink day and night because it creates abundant life. The effects of God's Word are not always immediately evident. It takes time for it to make its way into the root system of our beliefs. You have to water your roots, or thirsty tendencies are going to pop up in your life. It is not good enough to have deep roots; they are thirsty and need the proper nourishment. When you are thirsty, you will chase after anything for satisfaction. This is when people church hop, relationship hop, job hop, friendship hop, bunny hop, all around without the ability to settle anywhere. They can't stay anywhere long because they are always looking for something that they can't satisfy.

In the parable of the sower, Jesus speaks of seeds falling on rocky ground, where they are unable to take root and wither away. Some of us have deep roots but we are still shaky in doubt and fear. This illustrates the significance of cultivating a heart that is receptive to God's Word and willing to endure challenges and trials (see Mark 4:5-6). Through faith, perseverance, and a deepening relationship with God, our roots can grow deep, enabling us to weather the storms of life and remain grounded in Him.

See, the problem with most church attendees is that they attend a HOUSE, but they are not planted in a HOUSE!!!!! In the grand journey of life, if you've found your place like a tree firmly planted in the ground, your foremost objective is to maintain that deep-rooted connection. To withstand the trials and tribulations that time will inevitably throw your way, you must build a robust foundation, one that requires an elevated level of teaching. This means opening your heart to concepts and ideas that may be entirely unfamiliar, ones you've never encountered before, and some that might even challenge the very core of your beliefs. The knowledge you've gathered in the past was undoubtedly valuable for your previous foundation.

It was like a shield protecting the essence of who you are. But as you progress through life, the battles you face in each new phase will demand a different armor, one that can stand firm when the storms of adversity rage.

> **THE PARADOX IS THAT YOU CAN ATTEND CHURCH FAITHFULLY AND BEAR THE ANOINTING, BUT IF YOU ARE UNTEACHABLE, YOU ARE UNCHANGEABLE.**

What you've learned has been excellent for the foundation you've laid, but it may not be enough to fortify you for the journey ahead. You cannot rely on your environment, nor can you rely solely on your church, to guarantee your victory. You must actively seek another level of knowledge, one that will reinforce the bedrock of your existence, allowing you to withstand even greater pressures that lie in wait.

Entering the next phase of the journey with an unteachable spirit is akin to trying to navigate uncharted territory with a blindfold on. It's a cause for concern when you've convinced yourself that you already know it all. God's wisdom isn't static; it flows as a living stream, bringing forth fresh insights with every ripple. You may have acquired new knowledge and revelations, but if your actions remain unchanged, it's a sign of an unteachable heart. It's like having a treasure chest of wisdom yet refusing to unlock its riches. How can one be filled with the Word but still find themselves defeated, consumed by anger, bitterness, or nursing grudges? The paradox is that you can attend church faithfully and bear the anointing, but if you are unteachable, you are unchangeable.

Coaches often claim they can work with anyone, yet they also understand that an unteachable spirit can render even the most gifted athlete ineffective. The same principle applies in life. No matter what you do, it's essential to discern the why behind your actions. Without a clear purpose, your efforts are like planting a barren seed, one that won't bear fruit.

Seeds, when sown into the earth, plunge into darkness—a realm of ignorance. To emerge into the light, knowledge is the key. And the gateway to knowledge is the Word. Without a foundation in the Word, the seed remains in the shadows, never to see the light of day. As you read the following story about Eliza. consider the importance of not allowing certain emotions, feelings, and thoughts to take root in your heart.

Amidst the serene beauty of a village cradled between gentle, rolling hills, there resided a woman by the name of Eliza. Once, her heart had been as open and inviting as the fields that stretched out around her modest home. However, over the years, a shadow had fallen upon her spirit, a shadow cast by the insidious root of bitterness.

Eliza's journey into the thorny thickets of bitterness had been a gradual descent, like a tree's growth, imperceptible until it overshadowed all that was beneath it. It began with a series of disappointments, each more potent than the last, and each one added another layer to the thorny cocoon that now enshrouded her soul.

The disappointments were like relentless storms that swept through her life. They arrived uninvited, leaving behind debris of broken dreams and dashed hopes. With each disappointment, the roots of bitterness delved deeper into her heart, entwining themselves with her once-vibrant spirit.

Bitterness whispered in her ear, a seductive but venomous voice that convinced her the world was a cruel place. It murmured that kindness was a fleeting illusion, a frail and fragile thing, easily shattered by the harshness of reality. In the dead of night, she'd lay awake, the tendrils of bitterness winding tighter around her, urging her to cling to her grudges, for they were her armor against further disappointment.

Forgiveness, once a beacon of healing and liberation, had faded from her heart. It had become a heavy burden to bear, a weight that threatened to crush the warmth and empathy that once defined her. She had forgotten how to forgive—the act of releasing her grievances seemed impossible—even though it was her own soul that bore the brunt of this unforgiving stance.

The village, with its rolling hills and friendly neighbors, had not changed. Nature's beauty still surrounded her, and the community remained a place of support and compassion. But for Eliza, the world had transformed into a desolate and unforgiving landscape, mirroring the bitterness that had taken root within her.

Yet, as with all things in life, there remained a glimmer of hope. It was a fragile seedling, tucked away deep within her soul. ***God always plants a seed of hope that has more power than any feelings of despair.*** If only she could find the strength to nurture it, to let the rain of forgiveness wash away the bitterness and allow the sun of kindness to shine once more upon her heart, then, just maybe, the spirit of Eliza could one day bloom anew in harmony with the beauty that surrounded her.

Sometimes we can't see the beauty in you, because of the darkness rooted in you. Roots have faces, and they show up after a while, making it difficult to regain a sense of control over your life. Maybe your roots are inherited from the environment you grew up in, the trees (family) you grew up around, or maybe it's a generational curse. One thing that I know about roots is that they will release whatever is in the soil they are planted in. Depending upon the soil, you can determine the quality of results you will get from the growth of the tree. ***It is important to watch where you are planted!***

Chapter 4

WATCH YOUR FRUIT

"But the fruit of the Spirit is love, joy, peace, patience, kindness, goodness, faithfulness, gentleness, self-control; against such things there is no law."
—Galatians 5:22-25 (ESV)

We learn from scripture that these are not individual "fruits" from which we pick and choose. Rather, the fruit of the Spirit is one ninefold "fruit" that characterizes all who truly walk in the Holy Spirit. Collectively, these are the fruits that all Christians should be producing in their new lives with Jesus Christ. These are nine characteristics of the Holy Spirit. This means that the only way people are going to see the SPIRIT is if they see the FRUIT. The FRUIT will appear as a result of the SPIRIT. It is difficult to experience the overflow and the fullness of the SPIRIT until God sees the production of fruit. There are nine characteristics of HIM, called the Fruit of the Spirit.

When you are a tree, and you are bearing fruit, everything that comes out of you should help a person live. Your actions and words should provide life. If what you say and what you do is tearing people down, killing them mentally, and harming them emotionally, then you can't be plant-based. You can't be a tree because trees bear oxygen, and oxygen provides life. It gives off what God gives off. So, when you are destroying people's lives, making them miserable, then you may be a dead thing.

> **YOU HAVE TO BE CAREFUL HANGING AROUND FRUIT THAT IS ALREADY DAMAGED.**

Most fruits and vegetables go bad because of damage caused by microorganisms such as bacteria and mold, enzymatic processes, or bruising. According to research, microorganisms such as bacteria and molds release their own enzymes as they grow, speeding up the spoiling process. This suggests that people who have been hurt, but not healed, release their own enzymes or toxic thoughts, beliefs, ideologies, assumptions, opinions, advice, and more into you when you are around. This begins to spoil your faith, hope, trust, expectation, beliefs, and the way you see others. You know when bad enzymes have affected a fruit because it leads to enzymatic browning or discoloration and, later, spoilage. When a fruit has been bruised, the bruising physically alters the exterior of your fruits and vegetables, which trigger enzymatic reactions. So, when a person is damaged, they have triggers because of their experience that lead to certain reactions from them. If you respond in a way that is not pleasing to God, out of character, or doesn't make sense, then maybe you have been the victim of receiving enzymes released from bruised or damaged people.

One healthy piece of fruit goes bad because it is in the proximity of a bad piece of fruit, or one that has been damaged. Damaged fruit damages good fruit. You have to be careful hanging around fruit that is already damaged. You may believe that you will come out okay consistently being around people who are damaged, but the truth is there is always residue left in your spirit. When a person has been damaged, it shows up in their language, inability to trust, love life, marriage, relationships, job performance, and the list goes on. Be careful because the word on the street is, "hurt people, hurt people." This is a true statement. This is the importance of allowing God to get rid of the bad parts of us so that we will not infect those people around us. The infection will affect the health of the overall fruit.

It is recommended that you select your produce last during your shopping trip so any fruits and vegetables that require refrigeration do not spend too much time at room temperature. We would refer to this as a lukewarm state, and we are aware of the revelation given to John of a people who would become lukewarm. God said that he would vomit them out of his mouth. They sicken God because they straddle the fence. You don't need to be tossed to and fro by all winds of doctrine. When you are easily swayed between opinions, doctrines, and beliefs, the way you worship is influenced.

In the Tabernacle, the presence of trees played a significant role, albeit in a context that reflects pagan worship practices. The connection between trees and pagan worship can be traced back to ancient cultures that often revered trees as sacred symbols of fertility, abundance, and life itself. While the Israelites were instructed by God to worship Him alone, there were instances where they deviated from His commands and incorporated pagan elements into their worship, including the veneration of trees.

One notable example of this deviation is found in the book of Jeremiah, where the prophet denounces the Israelites' idolatrous practices. Jeremiah speaks of the people constructing "Asherah poles" and setting them up beside altars dedicated to Baal, the Canaanite god associated with fertility and agriculture. These Asherah poles, often represented by wooden poles or trees, were regarded as symbols of the goddess Asherah, who was believed to bring blessings and prosperity.

The worship of Asherah and Baal involved rituals and ceremonies centered around these erected trees. Baal was a male spirit, and Asherah was a statue known as the female counterpart of Baal. Whenever Baal wants to give birth to something in the church, he gets into a relationship with Asherah. The two spirits will birth a spirit that will rule a church, a community, a state, or even a nation. The spirit of perversion is ruling in the United States. This spirit is a spirit that will take something wrong and try to make it right. For example, the spirit of perversion will take a woman and turn her into a man, and then force you to accept that as right. This suggests that

God makes mistakes when he creates us and that He is the author of confusion.

The Israelites would gather in groves or high places, often under the shade of these trees, to offer sacrifices, make offerings, and engage in various acts of worship. So in pagan worship, they would take parts of a tree and place them at the altar. This was symbolic of replacing the sons and daughters of God who are supposed to be like a tree planted by the rivers of water. They would have them plant these trees there during worship because worship represents the time of intimacy. Intimacy is the time when a woman receives the seed of a man to reproduce. So, the devil knows that if he is going to birth something in the church, he will cause the people to get into worship that is perverted—to give birth to the spirit of perversion.

Pagan worshippers believed that these rituals would ensure favorable harvests, bountiful crops, and overall prosperity. This spirit of Baal will bless you to blind you. He will give you rights in perversion, make you worship or accept something that goes against God, and then call it right.

> *"You shall not plant any tree as an Asherah beside the altar of the Lord your God that you shall make."*
> —Deuteronomy 16:21 (ESV)

However, it is important to note that such practices were in direct violation of God's commands. Throughout the scriptures, God repeatedly condemned the worship of idols and the participation in pagan rituals. He demanded exclusive devotion and worship from His people, urging them to tear down these idols and remove all traces of pagan worship from their midst.

The significance of trees in these pagan worship practices lies in the distortion of God's intended symbolism. Trees, in their natural state, are beautiful representations of God's creation, providing shade, shelter, and sustenance. In the Bible, trees are often used as positive symbols, representing righteousness, stability, and spiritual growth. However, when trees were erected as objects of worship in pagan rituals, they became a perversion of God's intended symbolism, leading His people astray and fostering idolatry. Remember we, as trees, are the same way. When we allow people to lift us up, glorify us, worship us as leaders, ministers, and prophets, among other things, we place ourselves on a dangerous path that will birth perversion. When we lead people to us, instead of leading them to God, we have made ourselves an idol, erected in the tabernacle. This is no different than Jezebel and Ahab.

> **WHEN THE ONE YOU WORSHIP DOESN'T SATISFY YOU, YOU ARE IN TROUBLE.**

The biblical narrative emphasizes the importance of worshiping God and God alone while avoiding the pitfalls of idolatry. Idolatry is not just graven images, but anything that is lifted above God. As believers, we are called to recognize and reject any form of pagan worship or idolatrous practices that can lead us away from the true worship of the one true God. The lessons from the Israelites' deviant worship serve as a reminder to remain faithful to God's commands and to continually seek His guidance in our worship practices.

The presence of trees in the tabernacle as objects of pagan worship reflects a departure from God's commands and a distortion of the symbolism that He intended. While trees can be beautiful representations of God's creation, their use in pagan rituals and idolatrous practices is contrary to the worship of the one true God. As believers, it is essential to remain vigilant in our devotion, avoiding any form of idolatry and instead directing our worship solely towards the Almighty.

This is why Jesus told his disciples that He needed to go through Samaria. There, He talked to the woman at the well. In the conclusion of their conversation, He stated that now is the time that the true worshippers will worship in spirit and in truth. So, the reason He needed to go through Samaria, was to restore the true posture and spirit of worship. He was letting us know that worship was not about a place or a group of people, but about our relationship with God. You can't worship until you are walking in truth. The woman at the well was going to worship daily but leaving unchanged. The cycles of her life reflected it. Jesus referred to her as being thirsty. She left still desiring something else, feeling like something was missing, not satisfied with the one she went to worship. When the one you worship doesn't satisfy you, you are in trouble. If you are worshiping Jesus for real, then you will drink from living water. Jesus satisfies me. When He satisfies you, you will keep coming back to HIM. You will keep showing up for Him. You will love Him through the rough times because you can't get enough of Him. He is my everything.

Chapter 5

DON'T BE CAUGHT WITHOUT FRUIT

> *"He is like a tree planted by streams of water that yields its fruit in its season, and its leaf does not wither. In all that he does, he prospers."*
> —Psalm 1:3, ESV

In the pristine Garden of Eden, where beauty and perfection intertwined, Adam and Eve found themselves surrounded by an array of luscious and tempting fruits. God, the loving Creator, had graciously provided them with an abundance of trees, each bearing fruit for their sustenance and delight. It was a bountiful paradise, a testament to the generosity and care of their Maker.

In the unfolding of time, the symbolic relationship between fruit and mankind continued to evolve. Throughout the pages of the Bible, fruit often served as a metaphor for the outcome of one's actions and choices. Just as a tree is known by its fruit, so too is humanity known by the fruit it bears. The fruit of righteousness, born from a life lived in alignment with

God's commands, is described as sweet and satisfying. In the Psalms, it is written,

> "He is like a tree planted by streams of water that yields its fruit in its season, and its leaf does not wither. In all that he does, he prospers."
> —Psalm 1:3, ESV

These words resonate with a profound truth: when humanity aligns its heart, mind, and actions with God's will, it bears fruit that brings blessings and prosperity to both the individual and the world. Conversely, the fruit of wickedness and disobedience yields bitter consequences. The apostle Paul warns,

> "Do not be deceived: God is not mocked, for whatever one sows, that will he also reap."
> —Galatians 6:7, ESV

Just as a rotten apple spoils the whole bunch, the consequences of sinful actions have far-reaching effects, impacting not only the individual but also the community and the world. However, the relationship between fruit and mankind extends beyond mere actions and consequences. It also encompasses the spiritual growth and transformation that occur within the hearts of individuals. Just as a tree progresses from a small seed to a flourishing entity, humanity is called to cultivate a spirit of growth and maturity.

In the New Testament, the apostle Paul speaks of the fruits of the Spirit—love, joy, peace, patience, kindness, goodness, faithfulness, gentleness, and self-control. These qualities serve as an indicator of the Spirit's transformative work within the lives of believers. As individuals submit themselves to the leading of the Spirit, their lives bear fruit that reflects the very nature of God.

To lack fruit is an indication that you are unsubmitted somewhere in your life to the Holy Spirit.

In the Book of Matthew, we find a profound teaching from Jesus himself. He shared a powerful metaphor, saying, "Every tree that does not bear good fruit is cut down and thrown into the fire" (7:19, ESV). These words encourage us to ponder the significance of our lives and actions. The message here is clear: being fruitful isn't just about accumulating material wealth, but it's equally about manifesting love, kindness, and righteousness in our deeds. In the Gospel of John, Jesus offers another perspective on fruitfulness when he says, "Every branch in me that does not bear fruit, he takes away" (15:2, ESV). This teaching emphasizes our connection with the Divine and the importance of producing spiritual fruits. Just as a branch thrives when it bears fruit, our lives find fulfillment in producing acts of love, faith, and goodness.

Ultimately, the relationship between fruit and mankind teaches us about the significance of our choices, actions, and spiritual growth. Like a well-tended garden, our lives can produce an abundance of fruit that nourishes, blesses, and impacts those around us. By aligning ourselves with God's purposes, cultivating righteousness, and allowing the Spirit to bear fruit within us, we become agents of love, joy, and positive change in the world.

> **JUST BECAUSE YOU ARE PRODUCING LEAVES DOESN'T MEAN THAT THE PURPOSE OF THE TREE IS BEING FULFILLED.**

James, the brother of Jesus, delivers a powerful message in his letter, stating, "In the same way, faith by itself, if it is not accompanied by action, is dead" (James 2:17, NIV). This verse underscores the idea that faith is not merely an abstract belief but a living, breathing force that should lead to productive, meaningful actions. It's a reminder that faith comes alive through our deeds.

Unfortunate news: *if you are not growing, then it is difficult to produce fruit.* This means anything not growing is not producing. This explains why we don't see the fruit. You can be a tree with no fruit; ask the fig tree that Jesus cursed (see Luke 13:6). At some point, the fig tree stopped growing because it didn't produce figs. There are, has been, and will be people who look like they are full-grown and mature. If you are mature and grown, then you will have fruit. In Luke, Jesus said that if the tree is not producing any fruit, cut it down. There is no need for it to use the ground if it is not going to produce anything. Some of us are just like this fig tree; we appear like we should have fruit, but when something happens, it shows the lack thereof.

That's why the Bible says the fruit of the Spirit is . . . If you say that you have fruit producing seed, then I expect to see you bear fruit. Maybe not the first time I encounter you, but after I encounter you a second time, I should see evidence of the type of tree you are.

There are many people like this in the body of Christ; they look like they are productive because they are filled with leaves. They are seeing some success in their lives, children are faring well, and there are no major issues happening around them. Thus, it appears that they are fruitful. However, just because you are producing leaves doesn't mean that the purpose of the tree is being fulfilled. The purpose of any tree is not to grow leaves but to produce fruit after its kind. A tree serves no real purpose without the production of the fruit. God placed each tree with a specific fruit to serve a specific purpose. Jesus said that when He returns again to the tree and finds it bearing no fruit, he will curse it to death. Our actions and attitudes should bear the fruits of love, faith, kindness, and righteousness, reflecting the transformative power of faith and a life lived in accordance with the principles of the Divine. These teachings remind us that true fruitfulness goes beyond the tangible and extends to the profound and lasting impact we can have on the world and the lives of those around us. Our fruit is often not for us but for others to enjoy the creative power of God.

Can people taste God's goodness when they encounter you? Or do you leave a sour, rotten, bad, or poor taste in their spirit after they leave you? It is healthy to consider other people's perspective of us when we enter a room. I always state in one of my training sessions in the education field that there are a few types of people: a person that people are glad to see coming, one they cannot wait to see going, or one they do not even care to be around at all. I would hope because of the fruit I bear, people would want to see me coming.

Chapter 6

PAIN TO GROWTH

"For the flesh desires what is contrary to the Spirit, and the Spirit what is contrary to the flesh. They are in conflict with each other, so that you are not to do whatever you want."
—Galatians 5:17 (NIV)

A fruit is the result of seed manifestation outwardly what was already on the inside. Remember the first manifestation of what is about to happen, happens in a place that you cannot see. You can't see the fruit inside the seed, but you believe that something is there, and it will eventually manifest. Many of us can't see what God placed on the inside of us; we too, like a seed, must believe in what we cannot see. Is this why we must have faith? God is saying that anything that He does, He does it first in the SPIRIT.

But WAIT, aren't some seasons meant for you to shed, lose what you have, or maybe to some degree die? There is a season where trees lose leaves, don't have any fruit, and maybe even look barren. Farmers suggest that you prune trees before the winter, so when the spring comes, it produces better.

Pruning a tree can have many benefits. The first and most important is keeping the people around it safe. This means that when you are living a tree life, you first consider the people who are connected to you, around you, and maybe even work with you. If you are not pruned in the right season, then those people will feel the effects of you growing out of control. A lack of pruning shows up in the following areas: attitude, mood, behavior, response time, wisdom, peace, and happiness. The tree will become cranky, irritable, agitated to the touch, and they will make a lot of decisions from their soul (will, emotions, feelings). All because the tree—I mean you—did not allow the farmer—I mean God—to prune your branches in the off season.

Dead branches are the result of a damaged tree, an injured tree, or a dying tree. A dead branch can fall from a tree at any time, endangering nearby people-relationships, buildings or location/destiny, and power lines—your anointing. Pruning not only helps keep this from happening, but pruning has other benefits. Pruning can change your look, but you have to know when to prune. Remember, it's important that any pruning (other than emergency branch removal) be done in late fall or winter, during the dormant season. It's during this time that the tree is least susceptible to harm that may result from pruning.

Pruning not only helps with walkways, but it also helps with traffic sign views. **Oftentimes tree limbs can grow in front of a street sign making it difficult for drivers to read**, which in turn has the potential to cause a disruption in the flow of traffic on the road. This means that if you are not pruned properly, not only can you cause yourself to miss important information regarding your destination, but you can cause others to miss their turn to get to their destination.

God intends for us to be fruitful in all seasons. In the parable of the fig tree, the author notes that it was not the season for figs to grow. However, Jesus still expected the tree to bear fruit when he needed it. I believe that it is important that we understand that from the beginning God gave us a command to be fruitful and multiply in Genesis 1. Jesus said, "If you remain in me and I in you, you will bear much fruit; apart from me you can do nothing" (John 15:5, NIV). This Scripture suggests that when we are fruitless, at some point, we did not remain in God. As long as we remain in Him, **success is a promise**. Separate from God, you will be unproductive and unfruitful. However, if you stay connected to the Vine, your harvest is sure to be plenteous. **What's interesting about a fruit tree is that it produces fruit, but the fruit is not for itself.** You must render your seed useless to you. That means there can be no secondary benefit for you.

> **OUR ACTIONS SHOULD INSPIRE OTHERS TO SEEK THE DIVINE AND STEP INTO THE HOUSE OF WORSHIP WITH EAGERNESS.**

A fig tree does not enjoy the figs. The figs are a by-product of the growth and nourishment of the tree, but the figs are not necessarily for the betterment of the tree. The fruit of the tree can either (1) bless a human that eats it or (2) fall to the ground to produce more trees. No matter how fertile the soil or excellent the ministry, if you don't plant the seed, it abides alone. However, when your seed is sown, it comes into a position to be multiplied back to you.

In the realm of nature, trees stand as remarkable entities. They are not merely silent witnesses to the world around them; they are active contributors, enriching their surroundings in multiple ways. As caretakers, it falls upon us to ensure that these natural giants fulfill their potential, augmenting the beauty of their environment rather than detracting from it.

Proper tree care is more than just an aesthetic concern; it is a reflection of our commitment to God's creation. After all, God wouldn't want us to tarnish His kingdom's appearance or convey a negative image of living a life dedicated to Him. Our actions should inspire others to seek the divine and step into the house of worship with eagerness.

In a metaphorical sense, our lives are akin to these majestic trees, imparting a unique form of beauty to the world around us. They should beckon people to come into the fold, to seek the nourishment of spiritual enlightenment. Just as trees lend an undeniable allure to any home, we, too, should add to the appeal of our spiritual haven.

As I ponder, I can't help but wonder—are we true "trees" in the KINGDOM OF GOD? Or do we merely have foliage, resembling trees but barren, incapable of bearing the fruits of love, compassion, and guidance? Are we offering genuine, life-giving support to our fellow brothers and sisters, let alone those who are not in our spiritual family yet? Can we genuinely contribute value to the world, becoming more than just a symbolic presence?

> **GOD'S PRUNING IS NOT ABOUT CAUSING UNNECESSARY DISCOMFORT BUT RATHER ABOUT PREPARING US FOR A FUTURE SEASON OF BLESSINGS.**

The analogy of the tree in our lives is a powerful one, reminding us that our actions can either foster growth and life or perpetuate a mere façade. It's up to us to ensure that the trees within us and around us are vibrant and fruitful, offering shelter, hope, and sustenance to all who seek refuge under their branches.

God has a plan to transform some of us into true, enduring trees. He's preparing to impart us with the strength to withstand challenges and deliver us from both people and situations that hold us back. This divine intention is vital because many of us saints rely on situational salvation. Our faith often ebbs and flows with our circumstances, tethering our spirituality to the ups and downs of life.

Just like real trees that require annual pruning, our lives need regular examination and adjustments. Neglecting this process can lead to growth, but it's a growth marred by fragile branches and reduced productivity. Attempting to force growth in the wrong season is futile; there's a designated time for development.

Spiritual pruning serves as a catalyst for spiritual growth, eliminating barriers such as habits, routines, attitudes, thoughts, and personalities that hinder our progress. Yet, it's essential to remember that pruning is not a painless process. ***When God prunes us, it stings, just as amputating a limb is painful but necessary to save a life.***

God's pruning is not about causing unnecessary discomfort but rather about preparing us for a future season of blessings. Some blessings we pray for might not arrive when we want them because we failed to undergo the required pruning in the right season. Pruning often involves letting go of things we cherish the most, and it can be a painful and even disappointing experience. Yet, it's a critical step on the path to freedom from suffering and pain.

The benefits of pruning extend beyond the pain. It transforms us, addressing our flaws and inspiring change. Some of us resist change because we're content with who we are, reluctant to give up anything. However, clinging to the old self prevents us from bearing fruit. It's akin to being full of foliage, a show without substance. We mustn't confuse a display of spirituality with its true essence. Attending church and putting on a show is one thing, but reflecting what God intended us to be is another. If we're not careful, this superficial show can replace the real fruit of spiritual growth. It's like having a form of godliness without the Word truly residing in our hearts. Our lives should be transformed by the Word, shielding us from our sinful nature.

> *"For the flesh desires what is contrary to the Spirit, and the Spirit what is contrary to the flesh. They are in conflict with each other, so that you are not to do whatever you want."*
> —Galatians 5:17, NIV

Imagine a tree swaying in the breeze, its branches dancing freely in the wind. Pruning, much like the wind's effect on the tree, is a crucial process that reduces the amount of leaf disease on the tree. How does this work, you might wonder? Well, pruning increases the flow of air through the canopy of the tree, creating an environment where disease struggles to take root.

Now, take a moment to consider the parallels between the tree and our spiritual lives. Just as pruning improves air circulation, we can find spiritual pruning beneficial. All too often, various behaviors, mindsets, and things we hold onto can obstruct the flow of the Spirit of God in our lives. These hindrances, like diseased leaves on a tree, prevent us from experiencing a more profound connection with God.

Have you ever found yourself yearning for a closer encounter with God, wondering why it seems elusive? It's quite possible that these blockages *(leaf disease)* are responsible for the disconnect. When we don't engage in the necessary pruning, we retain branches in our lives that should have been removed in another season. These branches, much like physical obstructions to a tree's airflow, hinder the flow of the Spirit in our spiritual lives.

So, let us reflect on the branches we may need to prune, not just in the physical sense, but in our spiritual lives. Removing these barriers paves the way for a more unhindered connection with God and a deeper, more fulfilling spiritual experience.

Today, let's commit to no longer settling for the mere form of godliness. The desire of the flesh opposes the spirit, creating an internal conflict that hinders us from doing what we truly desire. Part of the Holy Ghost's work is to prune, sanctify, and purify us from sin. Just as God cursed the fig tree for bearing leaves but no fruit, we must reflect on what it means to be a tree in God's eyes. Having leaves is not enough; we must bear fruit to fulfill our purpose. If there's foliage without fruit, it's nothing more than a show, a facade that falls short of divine intention.

Chapter 7

WHAT'S GROWING IN YOUR GARDEN?

"The wicked man does deceptive work, But he who sows righteousness shall reap a sure reward."
—Proverbs 11:8, author paraphrase

The kingdom of God operates very much like a garden. What you sow is what you are going to reap. If you are not getting much out of life, it may be because you are not putting much into it. I believe the phrase is "You reap what you sow."

> **IF YOU WANT TO CHANGE WHAT YOU ARE REAPING, YOU HAVE TO CHANGE WHAT YOU ARE SOWING.**

The very first law to receive a harvest is planting a seed. This may seem like an obvious principle, but many Christians miss it. Too many Christians live their entire lives without understanding that giving (planting) finances is essential to receiving finances from God. No matter how fertile the soil or excellent the ministry, if you don't plant the seed, it abides alone. However, when your seed is sown, it comes into a position to be multiplied back to you.

> *"And God said, 'Let the earth bring forth grass, the herb yielding seed, and the fruit tree yielding fruit after his kind, whose seed is in itself, upon the earth:' and it was so."*
> —Genesis 1:11, KJV

God created the tree with fruit: What's interesting about a fruit tree is that it produces fruit, but the fruit is not for itself. A fig tree does not enjoy the figs. The figs are a by-product of the growth and nourishment of the tree, but the figs are not necessarily to the betterment of the tree. The fruit of the tree can either (1) bless a human that eats it or (2) fall to the ground to produce more trees. How can we apply this? Well, the application is simple. God has blessed us, but not just for us. We must not be so selfish as to neglect to produce fruit on the earth. We are blessed to be a blessing to someone else, who can in turn bring forth more fruit.

> *"Unless a kernel of wheat falls to the ground and dies, it remains only a single seed. But if it dies, it produces many seeds."*
> —John 12:24 (NIV)

Christians often make the mistake of giving with strings attached. Now keep in mind that expecting something in return for your seed sown is not wrong. That is the way God planned seedtime and harvest. However, too many Christians want to purchase books or tapes, mistakenly thinking that they will reap a financial return from this spent seed. Purchasing something from a church or ministry is not the same as giving an offering to God.

> **WE HAVE TO STAY IN THE PRESENCE OF THE SON, LOOK UP TO THE SON, AND GROW TOWARDS THE SON.**

The fruit contains seed and the seed contains more trees: God placed the seed of the tree in the fruit. A fruit tree that does not produce fruit will never produce more trees. A fruitless fruit tree can look strong, tall, and full of leaves, but it has no legacy because it failed to reproduce the seed that it received to create itself. A fruitless fruit tree is selfish and a poor testimony. The true prosperity of the tree comes when the tree produces fruit for others to enjoy and for the reproduction of more trees:

God gave apple trees apples. God placed apple seeds inside of the apples. God also placed more apple trees inside of the apple seeds. The legacy of the apple tree is inside of the apple seed.

Nothing can understand the viewpoint of a mature tree unless they are one. Trees take in the bad stuff and produce the good stuff—they take our carbon dioxide and produce oxygen. What they put out is for others to use. We are the same way; you and I have to take the bad stuff in our lives and still produce good from it. What we go through should not turn us into victims, but creators. Paul said in Romans that all things work together for the good of those who love the Lord (see Romans 8:28). You are never a victim, but always a victor. The difference in the two outcomes is perspective. When your perspective is wrong, you have to run to the presence of the SUN, so that he can show you a viewpoint from another dimension. Trees depend on the sun, look up to the sun, and grow towards the sun. This should be your same pattern with the SON. We have to stay in the presence of the SON, look up to the SON, and grow towards the SON.

In the cycle of sowing and harvesting, there's a fundamental truth that often gets overlooked—the waiting period. Just as a farmer doesn't plant seeds one day and expect a bountiful harvest the next, we too must understand the significance of patience in the process. Trees don't grow overnight, and neither do you. Your walk with God is a process. This is the importance of true discipleship. The disciples all had to walk with Jesus for some time before they understood how to live for Him and become his agent in the earth.

Just like we take time to grow, so does the seed that we plant in the ground of our lives. The trouble arises when impatience gets the best of us, and we start expecting to reap the fruits of our labor in the very season we've sown. It's as if we're trying to defy the natural order of things. But, in truth, it doesn't work that way. When we sow in one season and hastily anticipate reaping in the same, we fall into a common trap. This approach leads to frustration and often forces us to abandon our efforts too soon. It's as though we give up not only on the idea of a harvest but also on the very commandment that tells us to wait on the Lord.

I know that many people do not like to talk about money seed or monetary offering, but we must address the elephant in the room. You can't get apple trees from pear seeds. Nor can you reap financial wealth from love. It is the law of seed and harvest. You reap what you sow. Let's clear up something else while we are discussing money. Your tithe is not your seed, it is your expected return to God from what He has allowed you to acquire. Tithing plays a significant role in the harvest equation. It's a commitment, a sign of obedience to divine guidance. And yet, many people halt their tithing when they don't see an immediate harvest. Your offering that goes beyond your tithe amount is considered your seed portion. It is the part that is not expected of you to give, but you choose to give according to the measure of your faith. But we should remember that just as a farmer tends to their crops over time, we must maintain our commitment to tithing for a proper financial harvest.

The concept of tithing comprises three different types. The first is the Levitical or sacred tithe, dedicated to supporting the temple and priests in the Old Testament. Then there's the tithe of the feasts, a provision for religious occasions and periods of vacation. This second tithe served a dual purpose, offering both spiritual and social significance.

There is a biblical law that emphasizes the need to sow in proportion to our needs, not our lack. It's during times when we face financial constraints that we should be the most generous in our giving. The story of Isaac sowing in a land struck by famine serves as a vivid example of how giving generously in times of scarcity can lead to a hundredfold return. If we study our Word, it reminds us that part of every harvest is ours to keep. It contradicts the notion that Christians should have limited possessions. The Bible makes it clear that God can provide more than enough for our needs and leave us with an abundance to share joyfully with others.

In essence, these laws reflect the principles of patience, commitment, generosity, and faith. They guide us in understanding the seasons of sowing and harvesting, urging us to remain faithful even when our patience is tested.

Chapter 8

SUCKERS

"I am the vine, ye are the branches: He that abideth in me, and I in him, the same bringeth forth much fruit: for without me ye can do nothing."
—John 15:5 (KJV)

I had about eight big trees that were on the line of my home property. My house sits in a valley. I call it Wind Valley because the wind has been the thing that has caused our property the most damage since purchasing our house. So, over the course of the last four years, every windstorm has taken out one or more of these eight trees. We only have about two healthy trees left out of the eight that were there from the beginning. However, when the storm destroyed them, I never dug them up or cut them all the way down. I didn't cut it down because I didn't want to accept the fact that there was no longer any hope of them being as beautiful and big as they were.

Time has passed by, and now in the place where the trees were, there are limbs, baby trees, growing around the place where the old tree existed. There are a lot of small growths happening around the tree stumps, some of which have grown around and above the damaged trees until I can no longer see the damaged tree. All I can see is the growth happening around it. I was excited to see all the growth around what I believed was void of hope. However, one day when I was leaving home, I was looking at the area as the seasons were changing. God said, "This is what we have to be careful of in this season. Trees (people) who say I'm growing around the place I suffered the damage. Eventually, if they grow enough, people will not see that there is a damaged tree hiding behind all the small growth." So I said, "Lord, are you saying there are people who are showing signs of growth in an area that is damaged?" The Lord said to me:

"Just because it is growing doesn't mean that it is growing right." Selah!

That statement right there made me pause and think about what He was actually saying. Jesus said "I am the Vine, ye are the branches." The branches are supposed to be connected to the tree. Those that are growing are growing, but they are growing displaced and apart from the tree.

You can't get so excited about growth that you can't discern the health of the growth. You can't afford your growth in this season to grow up WRONG. This is a good place to make a note. Don't be focused on the growth but pay attention to how its growing. If it is growing apart from the tree, then it is a danger to the tree and anything in the yard.

I looked up the name of these growths, and they are called SUCKERS. They are called suckers because they zap water and nutrients from the main tree. A tree grows SUCKER because it is under STRESS. Suckers are a tree's attempt to grow more branches, often in response to some kind of injury. Where the SUCKERS grow will indicate where the damage is. If the roots have been damaged, suckers may grow from the base of the trunk. If suckers grow higher on the trunk, they're called watersprouts, and they are usually at the site of a pruning wound, a crack, or some other damage. This is an indication that they have stolen the tree's water to grow.

> **The devil is not afraid of you hearing a WORD because he comes to steal it after you have heard it.**

It's intriguing how these natural processes can mirror spiritual truths. Just like the suckers siphon off the tree's water, the devil often attempts to steal the Word of God from us after we've heard it. Oftentimes you hear speakers make a correlation between the water and the WORD of God. The devil is not afraid of you hearing a WORD because he comes to steal it after you have heard it. The devil knows if you RECEIVE the WORD, the stronger your root system. The Word of God is like water to our faith, and the devil understands that if we embrace it, our spiritual foundation grows stronger, increasing our chances of resurrection and transformation.

In the world of spirituality and growth, there's a profound connection between our roots and the power of resurrection.

To understand this concept, we can draw a parallel between a plant and our spiritual journey. Consider a plant with deep, strong roots. These roots serve as the foundation, anchoring the plant securely to the ground. They provide stability, nourishment, and a connection to the life force below. In a way, these roots represent our spiritual foundation.

In the same manner, we, as individuals seeking spiritual growth, need to have roots deeply embedded in a supportive environment. It's essential to be part of a church community with strong, healthy roots. Just as a plant relies on its roots for sustenance, we depend on our spiritual foundation for support and guidance.

The idea is that by being connected to a church with strong roots, we gain access to the life force, much like the plant's roots draw from the earth. This connection empowers us and provides the strength needed to rise and grow in our faith. However, how we grow is equally crucial. We must be mindful of whether we grow separately, detached from the collective, or if we grow while remaining firmly attached to the original source of our faith—the "vine," which symbolizes Jesus. Recall when He stated, "I AM THE VINE, YE ARE THE BRANCHES."

This analogy emphasizes the importance of staying connected to God as well as to the roots of our faith, whether individually or as a community. It's a reminder that our spiritual growth is intrinsically linked to our foundation and the support system we choose to be a part of. In essence, it underscores the significance of nurturing our roots to rise, thrive, and remain firmly connected to the source of our faith.

Allow me to recount an intriguing story about the day I discovered grass sprouting in my pool. The sheer audacity of it left me astounded. I decided to add an above ground pool to my house. In order to install it properly, someone had to excavate the land, level the area, remove all problem areas, and add two truckloads of sand. After all the prep, the installer placed the pool liner, similar to a tarp, in the frame of the pool walls. After the installation, we filled the pool with water. After one year with the pool, I discovered we had grass growing in the pool.

I asked myself a question: how on earth did this grass manage to push through the layers of earth, the weighty burden of sand, the tarp, and even the pool's solid base? It's essential to note that the pool liner was enduring the immense pressure of thousands of pounds of water pressing down upon it.

The answer I received was unexpectedly profound: ***the grass was chasing after the water***. It discerned the presence of this life-giving liquid, and like a determined pursuer, it refused to let anything hinder its quest to reach the water source.

This narrative serves as a striking metaphor for the disparities between the religious spirit, the spirit of the church, and the culture of poverty. In many instances, we permit various excuses and obstacles to deter us from seeking the Word. We concoct justifications for our absence, even when the Word is within our grasp. But God imparted a revelation to me—a reminder that people are on their way back to the Kingdom of God, not for mere entertainment or a show, but because they sense the presence of the life-giving water. The Word is their lifeline, and nothing and no one will impede their journey to attain it. It may entail time, endurance, and even some pain, but their unwavering determination will see them through.

I used to think that the grass managed to break through because the pool was constructed cheaply or that the liner was flimsy. However, God unveiled a profound truth to me. *When grass embarks on its relentless quest for water, it gains a supernatural strength—determination.* This determination knows no bounds and defies conventional limitations. Supernatural strength shows up not when we are strong, but when we are weak. The Bible lets us know that when we are weak, He is made strong in us. Therefore, we get God's strength when we run out of our own. This happens when things look impossible, when we are hopeless, out of choices, can't see our way through, or just physically weak. This divine strength manifests in a spirit of determination.

Determination, my friends, is the driving force behind every breakthrough. Picture this: the grass, against all odds, pushed through the crushing weight, defied the darkness, and broke through even when it couldn't see its way forward. It pressed on relentlessly, fully aware that the obstacle standing in its way of reaching the water would ultimately surrender to its unyielding pressure. The grass refused to succumb to the pool's oppressive force. SELAH!

What am I saying? If the grass didn't give up, it succeeded. You shouldn't give in to the pressure, no matter how tough it may seem. Don't throw in the towel. I understand that poverty and lack have tried to wear you down, and your faith has been hanging by a thread. Yes, I know, you don't have any one, you're in this alone, no one understands. God intended for it to be this way so he could give you His strength. Guess what, I'd rather you be weak in self but strong in Him. Through Christ, the Word says, you can do all things.

> **Every word is a seed, and nothing stops the growth of a seed that is running for water.**

So, keep applying the pressure, stay determined, don't accept the denial, and watch that which has been holding you back give in to your resolve. Your breakthrough is on the horizon! A wall never kept God's people out; it only a closed mouth. A mountain never blocked a disciple; it only a closed mouth. A sickness never held a child of God down; it only a closed mouth. You have to open your mouth and use your words. Reach for the WORD of GOD, and watch failure turn to success. Every word is a seed, and nothing stops the growth of a seed that is running for water.

But here's the kicker: how did the grass manage to grow through such adversity? Well, it turns out that during its growth stage, the grass develops an upward-reaching, needle-like point—a formidable force capable of penetrating even asphalt. So, you might wonder if all this is just about water and nourishment.

The answer, my friends, is no. The reason for that needle-like point goes beyond the quest for water. It's a telltale sign that the grass is, in fact, reaching for something greater. ***The ultimate goal is to get to the Sun***, and to reach it, the grass understands that it must pierce through every obstacle in its path. I thought that it was after the Water, but it is the water that gives them the assurance that the Sun is near. It's an extraordinary testament to the power of determination and a poignant metaphor for our own relentless pursuit of the SON.

Grass, my friends, has a knack for transformation. It changes its very appearance, alters its shape, and toughens up because the journey ahead won't be a walk in the park. It's a challenging process, but it's entirely feasible as long as you carry that unyielding determination to reach the ultimate goal. But here's the catch: you won't reach that goal until you're willing to embrace change. Change isn't just about your external appearance; it's about adjusting your attitude, refining your thoughts, treating people differently, choosing your companions wisely, altering your actions, and even revising your prayer and worship habits. The path to your destination is blocked as long as you resist change.

When I delved deeper into the subject, I discovered that grass can indeed break through concrete or asphalt, let alone a pool liner. When grass encounters obstacles on its journey, it doesn't just change its physical form; it sometimes needs to adjust its approach, altering its direction. Perhaps, you're approaching your situation from the wrong angle, or your interactions with others need a new perspective. You've been doing things the same way for years, with no significant changes. The key might be to alter your position.

"*A changed position reflects in a shift in character.*"

Here's the deal: you can't control what people think about you or what they say about you. Lies may have been spread about you, but what you have absolute control over is your character. If you diligently work on shaping your character, your reputation will naturally follow suit. Remember, a lie cannot stand the test of time when you outlive it. Your character is the powerful antidote to dispel falsehoods. Don't let the lack of character in others cloud your judgment. You may not change how others view you, but by focusing on character development, you can rise above it all.

This is the key, my friends—chase the water, pursue the Word, and what's bound to follow is nothing short of inexorable growth. Believe me, you'll reach your destination, make it through, and not just survive, but thrive. What did this resilient grass teach me? Growth is a choice, plain and simple. If you've stagnated for five years, ten years, one year, or even just six months, it's not because you can't grow, but because you don't want to.

If grass can break through all those obstacles, endure the pain and pressure, carry the weight, and persist in growing towards the sun, then so can you. But there's a catch: you must be willing to embrace change. God is on the verge of breathing new life into your professional endeavors. Whether you work at McDonald's, in a bank, as an educator, or as an accountant, I challenge you to aim for excellence and efficiency. ***Success is*** *a path you navigate by consistently going above and beyond, not by doing the bare minimum.*

The culture of poverty may say it's okay to cut corners, serve cold food, return too much change, half-clean restrooms, or even doze off at work, but when you're filled with the Holy Ghost, it won't let you rest on your gluteus maximus. Don't misuse the anointing; instead, channel it toward receiving above-average reviews from your supervisor. If you desire above-average rewards, then you must deliver an above-average performance. God is on the cusp of breaking you free from the confines of being a "bare minimum" employee, cashier, teacher, or line worker.

Get ready for promotions, pay raises, new job titles, and fresh positions. Stop griping about your current situation; instead, bring your best to the table. Don't roll your eyes at your coworkers or give your boss an attitude when you expect God's best. Remember, God's Word says that if you're faithful in little things, you'll be made ruler over many (see Matthew 25:23). Whether it's being faithful in the toilets, the fryer, or answering phones, God will eventually entrust you with greater responsibilities and blessings.

So, what's been holding you back? It's time to break free from "Lodabar"—the land of no pasture, no word, and no thing. You've lingered here long enough, and God is primed to lead you out to greater growth.

> **Don't let poverty dictate your destiny. It's not your inheritance; it's your adversary.**

Chapter 9

BUILT TO SUCSEED

"Do not think that I came to destroy the Law, or the Prophets, I did not come to destroy but to fulfill."
—Matthew 5:17 (NKJV)

Spiritual laws come with inherent consequences, a truth encapsulated in the well-known adage: "The wages of sin is death." When Adam and Eve were instructed not to eat from the forbidden tree, they were warned that the day they partook of its fruit, death would surely follow. It wasn't a matter of God arbitrarily deciding to end their lives; rather, the consequence was intrinsic to breaking the law.

In essence, disobedience carries its own set of rightful consequences. It's a fundamental principle that leaves judgment in our hands, for when we transgress a spiritual law, we're already aware of the impending punishment. The law itself dictates the outcome, making it a matter of choice rather than divine imposition.

Everything on the earth is in relationship with something that their life depends on to live. Fish have a relationship with water, and they need water to stay alive. A tree has a relationship with the soil. If the tree breaks the relationship with the soil, then God doesn't have to kill the tree; the broken relationship will do it for them. Did you know that humans have a relationship with trees? Trees need carbon dioxide in order to survive, and humans need oxygen to live. Humans don't produce oxygen; they produce carbon dioxide. Trees produce oxygen but need carbon dioxide. This means that God created trees and MANKIND to be dependent on one another. There are laws of relationship that govern the Earth. We must protect relationships that feed us what we need to live.

Trees have a relationship to water. They have to draw from water in order to survive. We are supposed to be like trees, which suggest that there is a relationship between man and water undiscovered. That's why the human body's composition is majority water. That's for another book.

We must uphold the law that governs our success. When creation is obedient to the laws and it stays in relationship with God, success will happen without anyone's help. Going back to the tree, as long as the tree stays in relationship with the soil, the law says it will continue to grow both naturally and physically. It will FUNCTION at its highest level and capacity, and no one will have to go back and check on it.

This is why you don't have to tell a tree when to shed because of right relationship with the soil. It sheds its leaves in the proper season, at the proper time. The law for the tree says that it can't go into a new year with old stuff. The Word tells you that you can't become new living as an old creation. So, you must be born again. When you are born again, old things are passed away, and behold all things become new.

So you, just like the tree, have to be willing to let the old leaves go, in order to grow some new ones that are designed for the new season. You can't keep all the same routines, relationships, habits, and mindsets, nor can you keep all the same friends. I said it, you can't expect to be transformed and remain in all the same circles and environments from your old life. You don't have to tell a tree when to change its colors. They may go from green to yellow or orange in the fall. Then, the leaves turn brown when it's shedding time in the winter. You see, there is an outer display of the inward season the tree is going through. Change for trees is expected every year. Why are we staying the same year after year? If you are living for God, you must know that change is inevitable.

> **YOU CAN'T JUST QUIT GOD; YOU HAVE MADE A COVENANT WITH HIM YOU MUST HONOR.**

Trees never get their seasons mixed up. They never miss a season. They produce when they are supposed to produce. We are God's greatest creation but can't even discern our next season. We can't handle seasonal changes. We want to remain in the same season all year. Every season serves a specific purpose and is necessary for the health and longevity of the tree. They never stop functioning as a tree. Even in their WINTER season, they are still a tree. Even when they are shedding leaves, they are still rooted and planted, AS A TREE. *They never try to become something else or someone else because of the season they are in.* Why does our identity change when we are going through a rough season? Why do we stop functioning in our call, purpose, and ministry because life is happening to us? Why do we look like something totally different when there is a storm? If a tree remains a tree, why can't we remain children of God at all times? Maintain your identity regardless of your circumstances.

Do you know why trees can maintain who they are without changing? It is because they maintain their relationship with the source of their life. We quit God like we are dating Him, failing to remember that when we are saved, we are married to Him. You can't just quit God; you have made a covenant with Him you must honor. Can I repeat something you have heard before? Why is God the first thing on the list to go when life gets tough? When we look at the things we can cross off our list to make our lives easier, He is the first thing that receives a time accommodation. Our job never goes, our friends never go, our time on social media never goes, but He struggles to make the daily cut. This is because our identity is found in things we prioritize at the top of our list, and not in God. This is why we keep changing because our relationship is not maintained in all seasons.

Finally, trees never stop producing OXYGEN!!!!! They function despite their storms, tests, and trials. They keep producing. WHAT if a tree were to stop functioning because of the season it is in? MANKIND would not have the OXYGEN supply necessary to live! We would die because of the law of relationship that we have with the tree if they were to stop producing.

Trees handle the sun, just like they handle the rain. Even when the winds get rough, trees fight to hold on to their relationship with the soil. They may rock back and forth, and they may end up a little bent, but they stay in the ground.

Think about that. This is why people are dying spiritually. They are not fighting for their relationship with their source of life. Instead, people are quitting, throwing in the towel, and they have stopped functioning in God. They are inconsistent with their relationship with God. We are the only part of creation who doesn't understand that maintaining our relationship with the WHO causes us to always be successful. GOD!!!

When a fish leaves the water, you don't kill it; he dies because he broke relationship with his life source. When a tree leaves soil, you don't kill it; it dies because it broke the law of relationship.

When a MAN leaves GOD, you don't kill him, HE DIES because he broke the law of relationship.

When Adam, in the garden, broke relationship with God, the only thing that could repair the broken relationship was death. This is proven by the above law. *This is why the Father's plan of redemption, had to be a Son's death, to fulfill the law.*

> *"Do not think that I came to destroy the Law, or the Prophets, I did not come to destroy but to fulfill."*
> —Matthew 5:17 (NKJV)

Death is the result of broken relationship or non-existing relationship with God. There is a law for sin. This is a LAW, not a rule—a law. *If anyone wants you to do anything that will break the law of your relationship with God, then they are after your success.* They are the enemy and a distraction from your success. When someone asks you to fornicate or commit adultery, the spirit behind the request is after your success.

So unless you want to fail . . .
You must recognize THE SPIRIT OF SABOTAGE!

Fish never leave the water, trees never leave the soil, but humans are the only creatures who walk away from what they need. Jesus said, I am the vine, ye are branches. Why fail? Why die because of a broken relationship with God? It's not necessary—and almost impossible—if you obey the law of your relationship. In JESUS, you have everything you need to SUCSEED!

According to Jeremiah 1:4-5 (NIV),

> *The word of the Lord came to me, saying "Before I formed you in the womb I knew you, before you were born I set you apart, I appointed you as a prophet to the nations."*

What is your purpose?

Jeremiah 1:10 (NIV) answers this:

> *See, today I appoint you over nations and kingdoms to uproot and tear down, to destroy and overthrow, to build and to plant."*

You're supposed to uproot anything that comes against your success. Then you are to build and plant more trees just like you.

DON'T EVER FORGET, YOU WERE BUILT TO SUCSEED!

ABOUT THE AUTHOR

Dr. Darius Jerome Williams is a native of Talladega, Alabama. In 2005, he received a bachelor's degree in English. Attending various universities, Dr. Williams returned for his bachelor's degree in mathematics, a master's degree in mathematics in secondary education, a second master's degree in educational leadership, a specialist degree in educational leadership and administration, and finally his doctorate degree in educational leadership, policy, theory, and research.

Dr. Williams has served in education for seventeen years across multiple roles—a math and English teacher, assistant principal, principal, and adjunct professor—landing him presently as the Founder of Reformation Academy K-12.

Dr. Williams is a licensed and ordained preacher, an Associate Minister for twelve years, and a minister of music. He is the Founder of the nonprofit organization DTAG Ministries (Determined Teens After God) and The Word Center Ministries dedicated to teaching and nurturing the spiritual gifts of individuals. Through both, he has had the privilege of mentoring and guiding youth and young adults through the complexities of life while upholding Christian values.

I am married to the love of my life, Mrs. Rebecca Williams, and have three wonderful daughters, Kailynn Jai, age thirteen, Karis Joi, age ten, and Kaslee Joe Williams, age eight.

www.ingramcontent.com/pod-product-compliance
Lightning Source LLC
Chambersburg PA
CBHW062119080426
42734CB00012B/2914